Published by Charleigh Monroe Marketing
900 Commonwealth Place #2144
Virginia Beach, VA 23464

Copyright (c) 2023 by Georgette Lopez
All rights reserved, including the right to reproduce this book or portions thereof in any form - for example, electronic, photocopy, without prior written consent of the publisher. The only exception is brief quotations in printed reviews.

Lopez, Georgette
Lash Artist Laws: The Code to Unleashing your potential and Mastering Your Mind

ISBN 979-8-9889259-0-3

LASH ARTIST **LAWS**

Contents

Foreward
Good Morning
Lash Artist Creed
Confidence
Creativity
Action
Commitment
Resilience
Improvement
Positivity
Good Night

Foreword

Written By the author of The Subconscious Adjustment

This book in your hand will discuss many important life teachings that not everyone is privileged to learn. Georgette has applied these powerful lessons throughout her journey as a Lash Artist. There are those that mcy have heard of these principles yet have not applied them in their cwn life. To know and not to do, is not to know. Take this opportunity with an open mind and inspire yourself to fulfill your life purpose while positively impacting others. I have been blessed to have known Georgette and personally influenced by her wisdom and kindness. Georgette came into my life at the darkest point in life, the death of my father. She was a stranger I had never spoke to and she was able to ccmfort me and help me take the steps to continue living. I am so thankful that I met Georgette twenty years ago. Georgette's mother, Marion was also an integral part of my life staying positive. My father had started teaching me about the Laws of the Universe, but he passed before I was able to fully understand. Marion was able to continue teaching me about the Laws. Georgette had grown to be a very good friend of mine. She would tell me what I needed to hear and not what I wanted to hear. She did an amazing job keeping me on track with my goals and staying positive.

We both knew how important our thoughts, actions and mindset were. It is vital to have positive people in your life that are encouraging you to pursue your passions and be the best version of yourself.

We eat food to feed our body. What are you feeding your mind? It is important to feed your mind daily.

This can come in many forms such as reading a book, listening to positive audios, daily affirmations, and creeds. Your subconscious mind runs 95% of your life. This is where habits, reoccurring thoughts, beliefs, values, emotions, and personality come from. When someone is in a bad mood over an extended period, you see that they have become a negative and grumpy person. It's like they are on autopilot. We want to train and strengthen our mind to run on autopilot but as a positive person. This will create a shield of armor from all the obstacles you will be challenged with. These obstacles will come in the form of people, events, and circumstances. It is critical to keep your positive mindset despite the inevitable challenges that come into your life. Nothing worth doing is going to be easy.

Georgette sees the importance of positively feeding her mind to creatively express her passion and creativity. Georgette has started a podcast, written a Lash Artist Creed, and written this inspirational book on the Lash Artist Laws. Read the Creed first thing in the morning, before you meet with your client, after you have a cancellation, before you go to bed and anytime you are doubting yourself throughout the day. Reading this Creed allows your subconscious mind to transform, truly believe in yourself, and work to become an unstoppable force that will achieve your dreams and fulfill your destiny.

You are one of the privileged that is going to benefit from the advantage of knowing the Lash Artist Laws. When you fall off track, read this book to reignite your desire to pursue your goals. Setbacks are a learning experience to refocus and tackle your dreams.
When you apply the Lash Artist Laws into your life, you will be forever changed. Keep this book close and read it many times.

-Linda A. Lawler

Create The Lash Artist Experience You Desire

LASH ARTIST CREED

I am a Lash Artist. A creator of beauty and a pioneer of expression. My artistry is original, transforming the ordinary into the extraordinary. I embrace my uniqueness. It is the foundation of my power.

The time to create is now– This is my hour.

In a world that may not fully comprehend my path, I stand firm in my craft. I am a visionary, a dreamer, and a believer in the magic of my creations.

In my artistry lies the spark to ignite transformations, both external and from within. I embrace challenges as stepping stones to greatness. It won't always be easy, but I am here to win.

I am an agent of change, inspiring others to embrace their own talents.

I am a Lash Artist. My purpose is to leave a trail of beauty, confidence, and empowerment wherever I go, it's all balance.

I believe in the boundless possibilities that lie ahead, and I pledge to think big, dream even bigger, and to embrace every opportunity that comes my way. With passion in my heart and tweezers in my hand, I am a Lash Artist – forever. This is where I stand.

Once a Lash Artist, always a Lash Artist

Good Morning

Not because you don't know the answer right now, means the answer does not exist.

REPEAT AFTER ME

I am a Confident and Professional Lash Artist.

Whenever you start to doubt yourself, remember you are the only gate keeper of your self confidence.

In a world that does not always seem suited for creatives, balance and harmony exists. Lash Artists have the ability to transform the ordinary into the extraordinary. The key lies in their confidence to believe in themselves and think big. Practicing Self Confidence empowers you to trust your instincts and take bold steps towards your dreams but you have to believe in yourself before anyone else does. With every lash extension applied, you are not wasting your time, you are lashing a vivid path to your aspirations. When you wholeheartedly believe in yourself, you attract others with the same confidence also. Doubts and fears may attempt to stop your creativity, but a confident Lash Artist will rise above the skepticism.

When obstacles emerge, because they will, believe in your ability to figure it out. You have your own personality, and lashing style. Trust that when you put that on display, you will attract clients that love your style and you will also inspire others to pick up their tweezers and start lashing. Confidence acts as a guiding light, leading you towards your dreams and aspirations. As a Lash Artist, you are gifted. Find the courage to always believe in yourself. Embrace your uniqueness and the power of your skill and you will allow yourself to step into the limitless reality of what you know you are able to achieve.

REPEAT AFTER ME

I am a Creative and Professional Lash Artist.

Dare to experiment in ways that feel natural to you and you open yourself up to a world of artistic growth and innovation.

Everything is connected. As a Lash Artist, you embark on a creative journey, seeking to create customized lash styles for your lash clients. Embracing your personal values, and harnessing the power of self-reflection is very powerful in becoming your most authentic and creative self.

There are infinite perspectives and possibilities giving you the ability to tap into your genuine abilities, and truest dreams for inspiration. True creativity arises from within so you are able to create from being attentive to your own thoughts, emotions, and experiences. Within your creativity lies the potential to reshape the world and inspire others to embrace their unique gifts.

Every experience is relative to your perception. Embrace what may be seen as failures in your craft, and instead see them as stepping stones towards improvement. By understanding that growth is a process, you allow your creativity to flourish at its own pace. Your thoughts and intentions influence your reality. Set clear intentions for each day, for each lash design. Watch your work transform into a reflection of your passion and dedication, resonating deeply with your true self you and your clients.

REPEAT AFTER ME

I am an Action Taking Lash Artist

Every action you take can inspire and impact others positively.

To achieve your goals and desires, you must not only dream and visualize them, but also take inspired and purposeful actions towards them. Your passion can create an uplifting and positive environment during each appointment, but use inspired action to continue your pursuit as a Lash Artist- acquiring both business, and clients. When you cultivate meaningful relationships with your existing clients and provide them with a unique and special experience, they will feel your genuine love for what you do. Constructive feedback can help you improve your skills and service quality. Encourage your clients to share their thoughts and be receptive to their suggestions.

When they see you value their opinions, it strengthens your bond and shows them you are committed to continuous improvement. Express gratitude genuinely. Let your clients know how much you appreciate their support and trust in your lash artistry skills. A heartfelt thank you note or a simple verbal expression of gratitude can leave a lasting impression and reinforce the emotional connection between you and your clients. Building these strong connections will not only lead to loyal customers but also a sense of fulfillment and purpose on your journey as a Lash Artist.

REPEAT AFTER ME

I am a Committed and Professional Lash Artist.

It's not a secret anymore. Practice makes progress

Every action has a consequence. As a Lash Artist, you are part of a dynamic industry and amazing opportunities can arise unexpectedly. When you consistently show up and take small steps, leaps, and bounds towards your goals, you set in motion a powerful effect that propels you in the direction of your goals. Recognize the importance of always showing up because it lays the foundation for growth and prepares you for the opportunities that can come your way. When you show up consistently for yourself, you begin to build trust not only with yourself but also with your clients, and even with your community.

When you are committed to your craft, you become more prepared to seize opportunities with confidence and competence – reaping the rewards of your persistence. It may be tough to show up sometimes, but don't underestimate the power of daily habits, or mundane routines. Intentional habits propel you in your desired direction. By taking small steps consistently, you create a larger compounding effect that attracts your goals straight to you. Your response to life shapes the outcome. When you commit to showing up, the more you will find yourself aligned as an accomplished Lash Artist.

REPEAT AFTER ME

I am a Resilient and Professional Lash Artist.

Use your free time to read new books, reflect, & journal

Life operates in cycles of ups and downs, ebbs and flows, challenges and ease. The Lash industry is no exception. Your journey is not immune to hard times or setbacks. Harness the power of resilience to appreciate the art of bouncing back stronger from the difficulties you are bound to face. There will be times when you experience your greatest successes, followed by periods of doubt. Understanding and accepting there is a rhythm to your career will help you remain grounded. From there, you become resilient. You become resilient when you endure challenges – When you reframe setbacks as opportunities to learn.

You become resilient when you adopt a growth mindset. It is extremely important to acknowledge your emotions. Feel what you need to feel, express yourself without judgement but also know that one day you will be able to feel them without being totally consumed by them. Join networks of driven Lash Artists. When you empower others, you are also empowering yourself. Treat everything with kindness and understanding. By practicing this form of compassion, you are nurturing your inner strength to empower yourself and rise above challenges with renewed determination.

REPEAT AFTER ME

I am Continuously Improving as a Lash Artist.

Celebrate your accomplishments but continue to practice.

When you apply your knowledge in real world scenarios, you will gain valuable experience and insights that cannot be attained through theory alone. I assure you, there is no such thing as failure. What you may perceive as a mistake, will become a stepping stone to growth. Perceived failures become opportunities for self reflection and constructive feedback. A mindset dedicated to improving inspires you to always believe in your ability to develop. That thought process is aligned with the constant flow of energy towards your progress and eventual transformation.

If you ever feel stuck, shift your focus from seeking perfection to celebrating progress, both big and small. Let each celebration become a source of motivation to keep moving forward and remind you that progress is a powerful force that pushes you forward on our journey. As you embrace continuous improvement, you align yourself with the universal flow of energy, constantly evolving on your path as an empowered and accomplished Lash Artist.

REPEAT AFTER ME

I have a Positive Mindset

Infuse gratitude into your daily practice

The world around you responds to your thoughts, beliefs, and actions. By embracing a positive mindset, you align yourself with success and fulfillment. Your thoughts are like magnets, attracting corresponding energies. Optimism is an essential factor in manifesting the career, client relationships, and growth you desire. By shifting your focus from the limitations, to the possibilities, you open up a world of opportunities. Your thoughts and emotions, are a sign from the Universe that you can still choose to believe in yourself.

Showing gratitude will always keep you showered with more reasons to be grateful. Visualization is a powerful practice to manifest your desires. Daydream. Allow your mind to wander, imagining the perfect career and success with vivid clarity. Feel the emotions your thoughts bring you. When you take the time to align your thoughts and emotions with your vision, you magnetize your dreams into reality. Choose to surround yourself with positivity. Don't underestimate good company. You will want a nurturing environment and a positive mindset to encourage your efforts.

REPEAT AFTER ME

I AM A Lash Artist

Good Night

It Was Within You All Along

Made in the USA
Columbia, SC
28 December 2023